creepy creatures

CONTENTS

Published by Creative Education
P.O. Box 227, Mankato, Minnesota 56002
Creative Education is an imprint of
The Creative Company
www.thecreativecompany.us

Design and production by Ellen Huber
Art direction by Rita Marshall
Printed by Corporate Graphics
in the United States of America

Photographs by 123RF (Adrian Hillman, Pavel Konovalov,
Reddz, Natalia Volodko), Alamy (John Cancalosi, Itani
Images), CritterZone.com (Andrew Williams), Getty
Images (Kenneth Garrett, Acha Joaquin Gutierrez,
Roy Toft), iStockphoto (Maximillian-Sethislav Andreev,
Evgeniy Ayupov, John Bell, Eric Isselée, Achim Prill, Dave
Rodriguez, Cindy Singleton, Alexei Zaycev), National
Geographic Image Collection (David Liittschwager, Piotr
Naskrecki/Minden Pictures), Shutterstock (Buhantsov
Alexey, Gerrit_de_Vries, David Dohnal, Sebastian Duda,
Robert Adrian Hillman, Kletr, Newphotoservice, StanOd)

Library of Congress Cataloging-in-Publication Data
Bodden, Valerie.
Scorpions / by Valerie Bodden.
p. cm. — (Creepy creatures)
Summary: A basic introduction to scorpions, examining
where they live, how they grow, what they eat, and
the unique physical traits that help to define them,
such as their poisonous stingers.
Includes index.
ISBN 978-1-58341-995-3
1. Scorpions—Juvenile literature. I. Title. II. Series.
QL458.7.B63 2011
595.4'6—dc22   2009052521
CPSIA: 040110 PO1135

First Edition
9 8 7 6 5 4 3 2 1

scorpions

VALERIE BODDEN

CREATIVE EDUCATION

You are helping your parents build a campfire. You pick up a big stick. A strange-looking creature scurries out from under it. It has big claws and a curved tail. It is a scorpion!

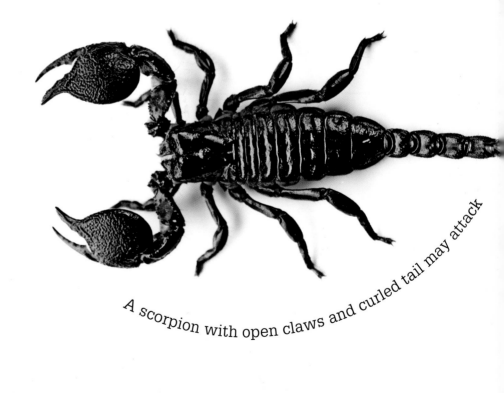

A scorpion with open claws and curled tail may attack

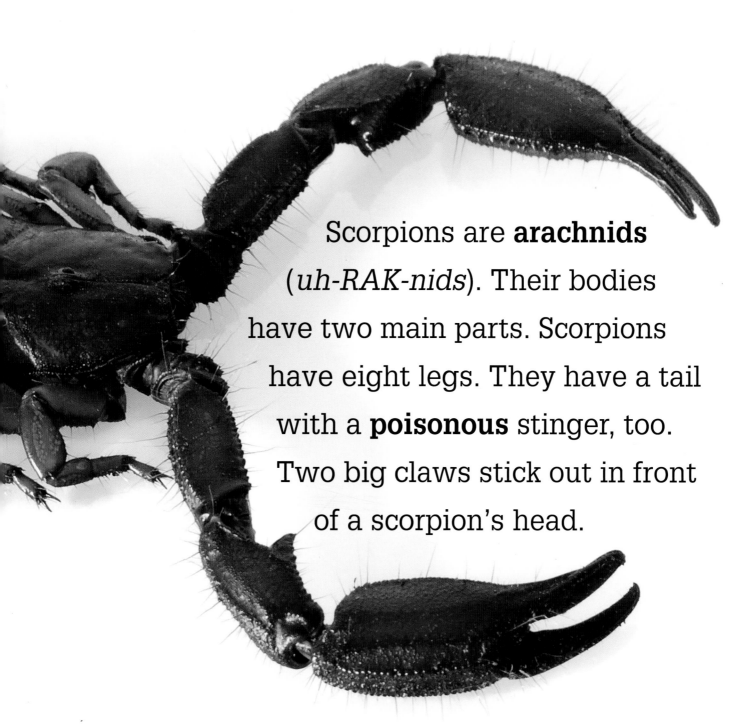

Scorpions are **arachnids** (*uh-RAK-nids*). Their bodies have two main parts. Scorpions have eight legs. They have a tail with a **poisonous** stinger, too. Two big claws stick out in front of a scorpion's head.

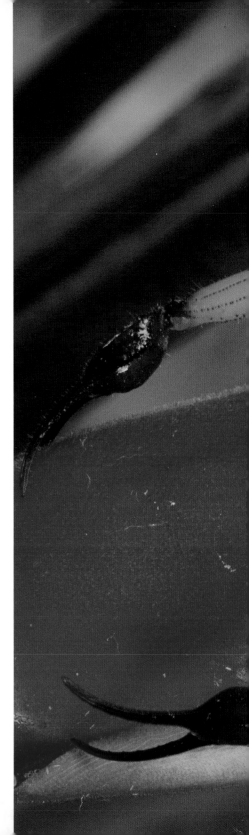

Some scorpions are as small as your little finger. Others are as big as a grown-up's hand! Most scorpions are brown or black. Some are yellow or green.

Many scorpions are more than three inches (7.6 cm) long

This scorpion is found in the hottest parts of the world

There are about 1,500 different kinds of scorpions. Striped bark scorpions can be found in many areas. Emperor scorpions are some of the biggest scorpions.

Emperor scorpions come from Africa

Some big lizards will eat even the most poisonous scorpions

Most scorpions live in warm places. They make their homes in deserts, rainforests, and mountains. Scorpions have to watch out for **predators**. Lizards, snakes, and bats all eat scorpions.

Mother scorpions give birth to live scorpion babies. The babies climb onto their mother's back after they are born. Baby scorpions look like small adult scorpions. As they grow, they get too big for their skin. They **molt** so they can keep growing. Some scorpions can live for 20 years!

A mother carries her babies on her back until after they molt

Scorpions will eat large bugs or mice

Scorpions eat **insects**, frogs, and mice. They hunt at night. Most scorpions sit still and wait for a small animal to come near. When an animal gets close, they grab it with their claws. Sometimes they sting the animal, too.

Scorpions do not usually sting people unless they think they are in danger. Most scorpion stings are not dangerous to people. But about 20 kinds of scorpions have poison that can hurt people.

Small or big, most scorpions do not have poisonous stings

Many people are afraid of scorpions. But other people keep scorpions as pets. People in Egypt used to think scorpions protected one of their **gods**. It can be fun finding and watching these big-clawed creepy creatures!

Egyptian pictures sometimes show scorpions (left, middle)

MAKE A SCORPION

You can make your own scorpion! Cut a large oval shape (like an egg) from a piece of stiff black paper. Cut four black pipe cleaners in half. Glue four halves to one side of the scorpion for legs. Glue the other four halves to the other side. Bend two whole black pipe cleaners into "Y" shapes for claws. Glue the claws to the front of the scorpion. Glue another whole pipe cleaner to the back, and curve it like a scorpion's tail!

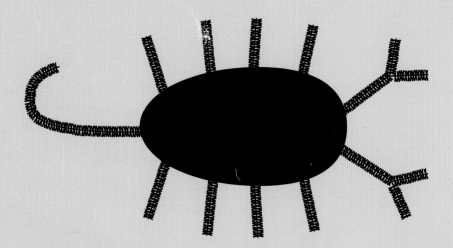

GLOSSARY

arachnids: small, eight-legged animals like spiders and scorpions

gods: beings that people think have special powers and control the world

insects: small animals with three body parts and six legs; most have two pairs of wings, too

molt: to lose a shell or layer of skin and grow a new, larger one

poisonous: filled with something that can hurt or kill other animals or people if it gets into their body

predators: animals that kill and eat other animals

READ MORE

McFee, Shane. *Scorpions*. New York: PowerKids Press, 2008.

Ripple, William John. *Scorpions*. Mankato, Minn.: Capstone Press, 2005.

WEB SITES

Enchanted Learning: Scorpion

http://www.enchantedlearning.com/subjects/arachnids/scorpion/Scorpionprintout.shtml

Learn more about scorpions and print a scorpion picture to color.

Stowaways Kids' Pages: Scorpions

http://www.landcareresearch.co.nz/education/stowawayskidspages/scorpions.asp

Learn more about the scorpion's body.